Communication

Important Tips For Dating Or Married Couples To
Enhance Their Communication

(The Secrets To Effective Couple Communication)

Ghulam Marriott

TABLE OF CONTENT

Chapter 1: Knowledge Of Conflict And Resolution .. 1

Chapter 2: What Exactly Is Conflict? 2

Chapter 3: Conflict Between People............................12

Chapter 4: Individuals Who Initiate And Sustain Conflict 18

Chapter 5: Communication Errors That People Commit Most Often 27

Chapter 6: Positive Visualization And Self-Talk.....37

Chapter 7: How To Express An Opinion, Agree Or Disagree 41

Chapter 8: Communication Skills..................................49

Chapter 9: Advantages Of Straightforward Communication..66

Chapter 10: How To Develop Confidence 70

Chapter 11: Never Evaluate Yourself In Relation To Others 80

Chapter 12: Identification Of Useful Information Sources 82

Chapter 13: Nonverbal Indicators And Their Influence On Communication 94

Chapter 14: The Building Blocks Of Effective Communication..102

Chapter 15: Utilizing Clear And Brief Language .108

Chapter 16: Observing And Displaying Interest . 112

Chapter 17: Advocate For "Window Of Soul" 119

Chapter 18: Reasons Why Relationships Fail 126

Chapter 19: Unspoken Regulation 151

Chapter 1: Knowledge Of Conflict And Resolution

To comprehend conflict and its ultimate resolution, we must first comprehend the nature of conflict. This indicates that you are able to identify a potential situation with contributing factors to the discord. It will also assist you in determining the optimal path to a solution, resolution, and ultimately reconciliation.

Chapter 2: What Exactly Is Conflict?

A conflict is a situation in which incompatible parties oppose an action. It is further exemplified by team members' divergent ideas and interests, which are almost antagonistic in nature. It can also exacerbate a mental struggle caused by external and internal demands with contradictory requirements, desires, and motivations.

When your principles or conscience are confronted by a situation that does not bring you serenity, there is conflict. This is evidenced by the medieval conflicts in which kings resolved their differences on a hill. Depending on the nature of the disagreement and the level of political tension, these conflicts were resolved through jousting or a full-scale war.

Internal conflict is difficult to decipher because it is frequently influenced by external events and how we assimilate that information. When someone does something that causes you pain, you may choose to remain silent in order to spare the other person's emotions. You may allow the incident to influence your thoughts and feelings about the person over time. Negative emotions and thoughts would have a chance to persist if you have a tendency to disregard the incident.

One can compare conflict to a container of soda. As long as it remains still, it is fine; similarly, as long as an incident does not affect you, you are fine. Then, however, something occurs, such as someone taking your parking space at the mall or your colleague receiving recognition for the work you've done, and the soda bottle begins to shake. However, rather than opening the cap to release some of the carbonated air, the bottle is set down and allowed to remain upright. Until the next incident...and the next...until the container explodes and the clean-up process becomes uglier, stickier, and more widespread, impacting innocent victims along the way.

Although being shaken is not always a bad occurrence, it is important to know how to respond to being shaken and who could be affected if your bottle explodes.

The Significance of War

Conflict in one's life is not necessarily a bad occurrence. It can foster growth and creativity and increase workplace productivity, especially if it is positively encouraged. This can include debates and competitions that encourage your teams to work harder and be more productive, thereby fostering team development.

Positive conflict also encourages you to seek out additional information to bolster your position. Your team will be determined to investigate additional options to ensure they have all the necessary data to make informed decisions. Conflict may also indicate that the original plan was unclear, resulting in confusion and obscurity, allowing for additional revision and clarification of the concept.

Conflict's Stages

The escalation of a conflict can be rapid or it can take some time to reach its peak. However, conflict does not arise without cause. There is always a buildup to the conflict consisting of five general phases. Each of these stages has its own emotions and distinguishing characteristics.

Latent Stage

This is when you are unaware of the potential for conflict. The conflict's elements are present but "invisible" to the participant. During this phase of the conflict, the issues are not significant enough to prompt a change, but neither party will be aware of the impending conflict until the other party expresses concern.

This stage may contain four categories of latent elements. Examples include when resources are scarce, seeking autonomy, having different objectives, and role conflict.

Perceived Level

The tension preceding a conflict is perceptible and alerts you that something is occurring. This is because the mounting tension became intolerable, prompting you to take action. This may take the form of an altercation or an explicit disagreement. During political outbreaks, this can take the form of non-violent protest actions or deliberate work slowdowns.

These actions may serve as a traumatic catalyst or be perceived as a threat by another individual. Often, these problems are exacerbated by long-standing expectations and strained emotions that have been endured for an extended period of time.

Escalating Phase

At this point, the conflict is obvious and thoroughly engaged. Typically, as the intensity increases, more individuals become involved. It is characterized by hard actions that are emphasized by patterns of hard-pushing tactics when the confrontation reaches its peak, and aggressive and argumentative words and actions. Retaliations are frequently swift and equally aggressive, and they may escalate into violence.

Escalation is inevitable and can occasionally be initiated by either side. This can enable the relationship's tension to be released and tempers to cool sufficiently to begin the next phase of the cycle. Engaging in the conflict may provide you with a new perspective on your relationship and enable you to make adjustments that will better the situation for all parties.

When there are conflicting objectives, when your team disagrees about their identity or a moral issue, and when there have been past events, conflict can escalate.

Aftereffect Phase

This is when the argument or debate has concluded and everyone involved has reached a resolution. Two outcomes are possible for you: either positive or negative.

A positive outcome occurs when everyone is satisfied with the outcome and can work together after the event. This is also the time when other issues are identified and resolved to prevent a new conflict cycle. In addition, it enables team members to challenge an issue that has been obscured by another conflict situation and to control the process with greater precision and knowledge.

If someone is in denial about the situation, the latent phase will last longer, and the escalation phase will be more combustible than if the issue were acknowledged. This is a negative outcome for the conflict resolution process.

Varieties of Conflict

There are typically three potential causes of conflict. Each has its own causes and frequently its own resolution strategies.

Task Discord

When working in a team, conflicts frequently arise due to the necessity of completing certain duties. There is frequently an issue regarding available resources that can create tension among team members. Individually, they will not always concur with the policies and procedures. As they interpret the instructions according to their own comprehension, there may be disagreements regarding the methods used by their coworkers to complete the work, which are frequently filled with judgments.

Disputes relating to a specific task are frequently a precursor to more significant issues and are frequently the source of further conflict. This type of conflict is frequently rooted in personal rivalry between team members. You can steer your team toward a resolution by focusing on the underlying issues rather than the surface conflict.

Relationship Discord

Relationship conflict occurs when team members disagree on a personal level. This may include their personalities, preferences, and dispositions. This is understandable when working with individuals who would not normally be in the same social circles.

The most effective method to manage this type of conflict is to organize low-stakes events that allow team members to socialize and discover their commonalities. These similarities can lead to improved working conditions for everyone. It also helps if you can act as a mediator between team members who are at odds.

Value Conflict

Depending on their political, religious, or other beliefs, team members may have divergent identities or values that lead to conflict. Despite the fact that people tend to avoid discussing these topics in the workplace, their values are frequently founded on them, which can cause tension among team members. Members may experience feelings of mistrust and defensiveness if they perceive that their values are under attack.

Again, the best way to manage this is to have your team members communicate as frequently as possible, share their ideas, and learn to respect their differences.

Chapter 3: Conflict Between People

When there is a disagreement between two or more team members, it is referred to as an interpersonal conflict. This is the natural consequence of requiring people with different personalities and beliefs to work closely together towards a common objective. This conflict can be emotional, physical, or professional and can involve a combination of home and work issues.

This conflict does not have to be negative, as it can help team members discover unexpected areas of agreement. It can also motivate them to find solutions to issues that have been challenging the team, resulting in a collaboration that would not have occurred otherwise.

There are six types of intergroup conflict:

- pseudo conflict — typically occurs in more intimate relationships, such as a marriage or between siblings, and consists of some teasing and tormenting

- fact conflict — when team members disagree about the veracity of information; • value conflict — involving the beliefs of various members and their awareness of another's values;

- policy conflict — when a plan of action or policy is questioned, causing tension among members • ego conflict — all parties are intent on winning the argument, with the ego playing a significant role, and resolution is more difficult to achieve • meta conflict — when members disagree about the communication process itself

Interpersonal Conflict Is Shown

It is crucial to keep an eye out for signs of conflict within your team, and the following are some examples of what to look for:

- Salary discussions are the most common source of conflict, particularly when a team member believes they should receive a raise while their supervisor disagrees.

- A team that must collaborate on a project despite members' inability to concur on its direction and unwillingness to make concessions.

- The unjust promotion of a single team member will undoubtedly cause conflict.

It is important to keep in mind that a team is composed of individuals with diverse personalities who will not always concur on everything, resulting in inevitable conflict. When this conflict is redirected into a creative outlet, the team is able to accomplish amazing things.

Discord Within Your Group

There will always be disagreements on your team. This is due to differences in personalities, priorities, understanding of the team's or project's objectives, and working and management styles. It is essential to resolve any issues as soon as they arise; otherwise, they may hinder the team's productivity. As a team member and, more importantly, as a leader, it is advantageous to be able to recognize and moderate potential conflict situations.

Well-managed conflict may have negative effects on a team, but it can also have positive effects. When a team experiences conflict, the resolution process enables them to work through the discomfort and find a method to build trust.

Team conflict typically arises for a number of reasons:

• Task-based conflicts — when a team member fails to fulfill their responsibilities.

• Leadership conflicts - various personalities will manage their teams differently, and not everyone will agree. By evaluating your own leadership style, you can reduce the likelihood of conflict within the team.

• Work-style conflicts—everyone has his or her own method of working, and the varying speeds at which individuals work can be a source of conflict.

Personality differences can generate a competitive atmosphere within a team, resulting in members supporting one another through difficult projects and stepping in when one member is struggling.

Conflict Avoidance

When you are aware of the triggers and employ a diplomatic approach to reduce or eliminate conflict in your team, you are practicing prevention. This includes employing a variety of strategies and activities based on the members of your team.

To reduce conflict to a minimum, you must encourage your team to communicate frequently. When your team is accustomed to communicating, misunderstandings are readily cleared up and tension is reduced, allowing for a clearer understanding of the project's objectives. Disagreements and misunderstandings will not flourish on a team where everyone practices forbearance, flexibility, respect, nonjudgmental attitudes, transparency, and clarity.

You must approach team conflict with a positive attitude and an awareness of your own emotional state. Ensure that you are sufficiently calm to address the issue if you are angry; otherwise, the discussion may spiral out of control and cause more damage to the team than good. It is essential that your attention remains on the issue and is not directed at anyone in particular.

Chapter 4: Individuals Who Initiate And Sustain Conflict

One personality on a team will frequently use tension to instigate conflict and challenge any proposed resolutions. In most instances, it is not the individual who will be problematic, but rather the manner in which they resolve issues. Their pattern is repetitive and comprises

• Placing blame on others — This team member has a tendency to place blame on coworkers or team leaders when things go awry. They refuse to acknowledge their own flaws, instead emphasizing those of others to detract from their own.

- They frequently see only their own solution to a problem as a viable option and are unwilling to consider alternative suggestions.

- Lack of emotional regulation; there will be intense feelings of dread, anger, and disrespect for other members as this person allows their emotions to run unchecked, frequently resorting to social media or the internet to express themselves. Even though the situation did not necessitate their behavior, they feel unjustified in their actions. The opposite end of the spectrum is when a person employs emotional manipulation to achieve his or her goals.

- Extreme behaviors, such as physical confrontation, disseminating rumors about teammates, stalking, or making unacceptable remarks about coworkers.

These individuals may struggle with interpersonal interaction, self-reflection, and change resistance. Eddy (2019) discovered a correlation between conflict instigators and certain personality disorders, including narcissistic, borderline, antisocial, and paranoid personality disorders. Despite the fact that these members may exhibit symptoms of these disorders, unless they confess to having a problem, they will not change, and you can anticipate the conflict to escalate while they are present.

It is best to avoid confrontation with them. Focus instead on how everyone can collaborate in the future. You can often anticipate when they will act out and take preventative measures. Unless the circumstance is toxic or abusive and you must distance yourself from the person, the following suggestions can be implemented:

- Show them compassion and respect.
- Evaluate the available options for managing your relationship with this person.
- Your responses should be concise yet informative, as well as cordial yet firm.
- When you control the meeting space in terms of the time and location, you can set the tone for the individual's behavior.

Discordant Conflict

When team objectives are challenged to the point where they cannot be attained, the conflict is termed dysfunctional. These elements would be present during this phase:

- Tension would increase; the team would have excessive tension, making them difficult to manage. This would enhance anxiety, hostility, and anger.

• High turnover rate; team members may not feel secure working with the constant tension, resulting in a decline in production and team morale as a result of their increased departures.

• Increased unhappiness—as team morale declines, team members become more dissatisfied with their working conditions, which impacts output.

• Lack of trust—team members may mistrust each other and management, decreasing positivity and possibly preventing them from interacting.

• Unachieved objectives — When there is conflict within a team, it may serve as a diversion from the team's outputs because more time was spent mediating disagreements than achieving the project's objectives.

As previously mentioned, when conflict is prevalent within a team, production suffers, which can have a negative impact on the organization as a whole. This would not only influence the company's revenue, but also its reputation.

Frequent Statements During Conflict

Even though the buildup can take some time, the conflict itself can be rapid, and the escalation phase can last minutes, days, or even months. During this time, attempts to find a tranquil path may be made, but due to circumstances or a particular individual, no resolutions are reached. This is also exacerbated by statements that can be interpreted as provocative.

• The use of "you" can be interpreted as an accusation and inflict a sense of remorse, causing the recipient to become defensive because they may feel insulted. When using "I" statements, the accusatory tone is removed, allowing the listener to consider that others are also affected by the conflict. Expressions such as "I believe the production delay can be remedied by working quickly." What is your opinion?

- Prolonging the discussion by bringing up past events or bringing up unrelated topics, thereby exacerbating the tension and prolonging the conflict.

Others are drawn into the conflict through rumors, gossip, or being duplicated on communication streams. When you notice that the conversation has strayed from the topic, delicately bring it back to the topic at hand, avoiding bringing up other people unless you need to address something said in a malicious manner. Remain focused on a single issue at a time, resolving it before moving on to another. It may take more than one discussion to get to the root of the problem, so patience is essential.

- Using "but"—when we use but, it nullifies whatever was said, making the person feel as if what they were saying is not essential or valued enough to be considered. Use "and" instead to create a more inclusive statement that not only validates the person's suggestion but also provides additional avenues to pursue.

When a crisis cannot be resolved despite all efforts, it is essential to involve a neutral third party who can objectively mediate the situation. Finding common ground is not simple and may feel like a 24-hour-a-day job, but with practice, patience, and dedication from all parties, it is possible.

Understanding what conflict is and how to recognize it is the first step in resolving it.

Chapter 5: Communication Errors That People Commit Most Often

When communicating with others, we frequently do things that undermine our efforts. People become defensive, shut down, and tune you out when you do the following, which utterly defeats the purpose of communication. But when you are in charge of your own emotions and clearly comprehend the needs of others, you can improve your ability to communicate with anyone about anything.

You commit verbal communication errors. The most frequent errors in verbal communication that most people make are as follows:

When conversing with someone, you tend to hijack the conversation with your own thoughts and emotions, rather than allowing them to communicate. As a consequence, your thoughts begin to wander to future plans or other concepts.

The second error is that you do not recognize their body language. When you fail to read their body language, they believe you are not attending to them. It is crucial to comprehend both verbal and nonverbal communication.

You commit Error No. 3 by failing to clarify your beliefs. When communicating with someone, it is essential to be certain of your intentions, and you must be crystal explicit about your thoughts. Otherwise, the individual will not know where their thoughts are, which will cause them to begin considering other things.

Fourth error: you lack empathy for them. They believe they cannot be open with you and share their honest thoughts and feelings when you lack compassion. As a result, they tend to close down and erect barriers between themselves and others, concealing their true intentions.

5. You lack a solid comprehension of their requirements. When you lack a solid understanding of a person's requirements, you are unable to communicate effectively with them. Without realizing it, you may say something that utterly offends them.

When communicating with others, we frequently do things that undermine our efforts. But when you are in charge of your own emotions and clearly comprehend the needs of others, you can improve your ability to communicate with anyone about anything.

You lack a comprehensive understanding of your own requirements. When you do not comprehend your requirements, you can develop feelings that cause a great deal of physical tension. Therefore, if you lose control of your emotions during an emotionally charged conversation, you may utter something that could offend or hurt the other person's feelings.

You are unaware of the emotions of the other individual. When you are unaware of the other person's emotions, it is difficult for them to explain how they feel because they cannot cultivate the same awareness of their own emotions in others. Due to a lack of understanding, individuals tend to become defensive about their emotions in this situation.

You lack a clear understanding of what you hope to accomplish with them. When conversing with someone, there are two primary objectives we must bear in mind:

Encourage them to disclose their emotions and opinions.

To enable them to recognize us for who we are.

To accomplish this, we must have a firm grasp of our goals with others and the ability to persuade them to join us in pursuing them.

We must ensure that we are progressing in our communication. Instead of simply requesting something, we must come from a place of desiring the other person's assistance and the best possible outcome.

Mistake #9. This is one of the most common errors in interpersonal communication. You do not have a clear understanding of the desired outcome. Both parties should benefit from the product. Otherwise, there is little sense in discussing it with them in the first place.

You lack a clear understanding of how to communicate with individuals from diverse backgrounds. When communicating with people who are different from you, you must be aware that they have a different way of thinking and feeling about things than you do, and they may require more time to deliberate over their decisions than those who share your perspective.

How can you best avoid making these errors?

When communicating with others, you must have a firm grasp on the following:

To comprehend how and where to communicate with them, you must be aware of their requirements. You must understand how and where they are coming from in order to impart information that motivates them.

When your mind and body are relaxed, there is no resistance between you and other people; they can immediately determine what you want and how you want it. When your mind is calm and in charge of your emotions, nothing holds back what desires to be expressed.

You must be intimately familiar with yourself in order to comprehend what you want from others and how to communicate with them so that they understand what you want from them, so that there is no misunderstanding between the two of you.

To comprehend how other people are feeling and what they are communicating, you must be aware of your own emotions; therefore, we must be empathetic toward everyone. To know what your needs are, you must have a clear comprehension of your own, and this is where we must ensure that our needs only serve others.

For us to know what we want from people, we must be aware of the outcome we're aiming for. The product must benefit all consumers. Otherwise, there is no purpose in discussing it with them.

You must be able to communicate with people who think and feel differently than you do because other people have distinct perspectives and emotions. You must be aware of this distinction when conversing with them for them to feel comfortable and open with you.

Now that we've enumerated the common errors people make when communicating with others, let's review the most important alternatives.

Here are two fundamental guidelines for interpersonal communication:

a) Others have requirements distinct from your own. When communicating with them, we must be aware of how they feel and think in order to comprehend where they are in their own world and be there for them when they need us.

b) Prior to speaking with someone, you must have a clear comprehension of what you want from them. It would be ideal if you had a well-defined objective to achieve and communicated with them in a manner that motivates them to take action toward that objective.

Mistakes in communicating with others are caused by a lack of understanding of how others think and feel, their requirements, the desired outcome, and the inability to motivate others through communication.

To communicate effectively with others, you must understand what they need from you and how they are communicating with you so that you can respond appropriately. To avoid these errors, we must be perpetually mindful of each of these factors. If we never have the opportunity to exercise and develop our communication skills, it will be very difficult for us to communicate with others in an effective manner.

Chapter 6: Positive Visualization And Self-Talk

Visualization and positive self-talk are mindfulness and relaxation techniques that can aid in overcoming stage anxiety and enhancing public speaking performance.

Visualization involves creating a tranquil or positive mental image or scenario. This may entail visualizing a tranquil scene, such as a beach or mountain view, or imagining a successful public speaking performance. By providing a sense of calm and control, visualization can aid in reducing anxiety and enhancing concentration.

Positive self-talk is the use of positive affirmations or self-encouragement to increase confidence and decrease negative beliefs. A person may tell themselves, for instance, "I am a confident and capable speaker" or "I am well-prepared and will do my best." Positive self-talk can assist individuals in overcoming negative thoughts and enhancing their public speaking confidence.

As part of a regular relaxation routine, using visualization and positive self-talk can help individuals overcome stage fright and enhance their public speaking performance. To obtain the greatest benefit, it is essential to identify the techniques that work best for the individual and to practice them regularly.

Seeking assistance from family, acquaintances, or a public speaking coach

In order to manage stage anxiety and improve public speaking performance, it can be beneficial to seek support from friends, family, or a public speaking coach. Individuals preparing for and delivering a public speech can benefit from the encouragement, motivation, and direction provided by others.

As a person practices their communication and works to overcome their anxiety, friends and family can offer moral support and encouragement. They can also provide feedback and enhancement suggestions.

A public speaking coach can provide more structured and specialized assistance. As individuals practice and prepare for a public speaking event, coaches can assist in the development of their skills and techniques, as well as offer feedback and direction. A coach can also assist individuals in identifying and resolving any specific obstacles or concerns that may be causing anxiety or hindering performance.

Seeking support from others can be an effective method for overcoming stage anxiety and enhancing public speaking abilities. It is essential to identify the form of assistance that best suits a person's needs and objectives.

Chapter 7: How To Express An Opinion, Agree Or Disagree

In order to have meaningful conversations, we will be required to express our opinions, request others' opinions, and then concur or disagree with them. Otherwise, it is not a conversation, but rather a speech or lecture in which we do not have a chance to communicate.

A conversation, according to its definition, is a two-way exchange of ideas and perspectives. The more proficient I become at expressing my opinion, arguing my case, and stating my reasons, the greater my opportunity to persuade others through conversation.

Don't use these two words.

Typically, we reason our thoughts using these two prevalent phrases: "I believe..." and "because..." It is not grammatically incorrect to use these words and phrases, but I believe there are better methods to convey my meaning. I challenge you to refrain from using them. Herein are my arguments:

When expressing my opinion, the phrase "I think" is simply too common and overused. To be an effective conversationalist with excellent communication skills, we must have a larger vocabulary pool from which to draw. Therefore, attempt to avoid using "I believe" since almost everyone else will.

Regarding "because," there are two reasons why we should avoid using it. Yes, it is equally as overused as "I think." However, there is a second rationale. The use of "because" in my argument will weaken my position and demonstrate a lack of confidence. Try it out the next time. You need not even rephrase your justification. Consider the following two examples:

a) I dislike drinking coffee at night because it keeps me alert.

b) I dislike drinking coffee. It keeps me waking at night.

Can you also perceive that the second assertion is more powerful? This is especially true when we want to offer advice or make a recommendation.

a) I do not believe you should not purchase this house because it is not located in a desirable neighborhood.

b) I do not believe you should purchase this property. It is not located in a desirable area.

The second example is considerably more confident and robust.

Because "because" and "I think" are so intuitive for most of us to use, it will require effort to refrain from doing so. Here are some alternative phrases for introducing our opinions, in lieu of the ones listed above. These are not the only ones; there may be many more. As long as tact and courtesy guide our dialogues, we can anticipate meaningful exchanges.

General Perspective

When you want to protect yourself or are requested for your opinion on a sensitive topic, it is advantageous to adopt a broad perspective. Sometimes, particularly in front of strangers, expressing our heartfelt or sincere opinions causes us discomfort.

What If Nobody Has an Opinion?

Occasionally, we simply lack an opinion. Sometimes we have yet to make a decision, and other times we simply don't care. These situations can be addressed with the following three phrases:

I'm indecisive.

This phrase is useful when choosing between various alternatives, but you need a bit more time.

A: "What do you suppose then? Will you purchase the BMW?"

B: "I'm undecided. Perhaps I should save money."

I have no opinion about this.

This phrase is beneficial when you are indifferent to your options and have no preference. It is imprudent to state "I don't care"; instead, it is preferable to say "I'm indifferent about this."

A: "Where do you wish to have lunch? Italian or Indian?

B: " I'm apathetic. You decide, I will comply.

Whatever makes you happy.

This phrase can be used when someone asks for your opinion on a matter and you don't particularly agree with it, but you can see why someone else might feel this way.

A: "Do you believe I ought to get a tattoo?"

B: "Do whatever makes you happy. I do not wish to acquire one, but you are free to do so. I will not pass judgment"

I frequently hear non-native speakers make the error of asking, "How do you think?" By inquiring "how," we are seeking a method, such as "How do you cook this meal?" The acceptable response to the question "How do you think?" is "I use my brain." Therefore, this question should not be used to determine what someone is considering.

Let's Agree to Disagree

I would like to conclude by mentioning this phrase. Whenever we engage in a debate or someone attempts to persuade us with their arguments, we may reach a point where we wish to end this line of argumentation.

"Let's agree to disagree" is a very polite way to let the other speaker know, "I understand what you're saying, but you're not convincing me, and it's clear that I haven't convinced you, either.

Therefore, let's end this dispute and remain comrades."

Chapter 8: Communication Skills

Babies begin learning to speak immediately after birth, expanding on their innate ability to communicate with their mothers through crying. Throughout the rest of their lives, a person's development and success depend in some way on communication, whether it be communicating with or receiving communication from others. While pursuing success, anyone can benefit tremendously from having strong communication skills.

The ability to communicate is essential to the survival of all living organisms, including humans. Obviously, compared to other creatures, human communication is considerably more complex and sophisticated. As a species, we utilize a variety of channels and instruments for communication, and so does every other species. Obviously, compared to other creatures, human communication is considerably more complex and sophisticated. As a species, we employ a diversity of communication channels and tools. However, interpersonal communication skills will be the focus of this article, as success in a variety of endeavors may depend on these abilities.

It is not a coincidence that the majority of large businesses and organizations incorporate communication skills training into their employee development programs. Employees with strong communication skills will contribute significantly to the long-term profitability and effectiveness of the vast majority of businesses and non-profit organizations. Employees who require specific communication skills, such as public speaking, may be sent to internal or external training sessions.

Few business professionals would dispute that enhanced communication skills increase your chances of success and the likelihood that your career will flourish in the future. Despite the fact that there are unquestionably other factors that contribute more to success than communication skills, it cannot be denied that they have a prospective impact. Learning how to communicate effectively is not the easiest task, especially if you have no idea how to approach self-improvement in general. Developing one's existing interpersonal skills and capacity for effective communication can be extremely beneficial for anyone. Developing one's communication skills will have positive effects, including an increase in one's home and workplace satisfaction and productivity. Increased connection fosters greater trust and comprehension, allowing you and those around you to form more durable and satisfying relationships.

As a result of the fact that humans are creatures of habit, many people struggle tremendously to improve their communication skills. Throughout infancy and adolescence, we improve our communication abilities. They require time to cultivate and adapt to, as they are deeply ingrained within us. Changing our tactics and methods of engagement, even for the better, requires stepping outside of our comfort zone and disarming ourselves against the opinions of others. We must abandon our defenses and plunge into the turbulent waters of life. It is a terrifying idea. People frequently find it challenging to give up the tools and safeguards that have prevented others from perceiving them as they truly are. They say that recognizing a problem is the initial step in its resolution. However, individuals are frequently unwilling to acknowledge that they require assistance or that their abilities must be enhanced.

The best place to begin when endeavoring to improve communication skills is with a thorough evaluation of current abilities and a determination of where and how to make improvements.

This procedure is best accomplished with a companion. Due to the fact that communication skills are acquired at a young age, it is common for people to have "blind spots" in their habits — areas or skills they lack but are oblivious of. Occasionally, however, individuals acquire specific abilities at a young age, and their personalities develop around those communication abilities to the extent that employing other abilities is equivalent to feigning to be someone else. Nevertheless, it is essential to avoid being antagonistic towards the procedure. Nobody is attempting to change who you are; rather, they are merely attempting to provide you with additional ways to express yourself. By developing your communication abilities, you may become more appealing, well-rounded, and emotionally robust. People can be quite different from one another, and their development process should reflect all of their quirks and eccentricities. Be wary of standardized templates for the development or evaluation of your communication skills. The crucial differences result from taking the less-traveled path; however, the final results should be the same for everyone, as a well-rounded set of communication skills should look essentially the same for everyone. Some people will have more to learn than others, and individuals learn in a variety of methods and at different rates. Some individuals may require additional practice to ensure that their skills are completely integrated into their communication toolkit. In addition, every individual will have different schedules and time constraints that must be accommodated for this self-improvement.

Communication skill development is a process of self-improvement, and as such, it has positive effects on personality, temperament, and quality of life as a whole. In certain instances, even the most fundamental "how to enhance communication skills" templates will be effective. Finding issues or contradictions in your repertoire of actions, words, tone, or grammar; identifying them; identifying situations in which you feel comfortable making changes (such as with your closest friends and family); and putting these new or unused skills into practice could be all that is required of you as a process. If you feel capable of doing so, it may be advantageous to solicit feedback. If not, be certain to monitor yourself closely as you make improvements.

As always, tolerance is crucial. Take your time; it may take you some time to develop the outstanding communication skills you desire. Self-improvement of any kind should never be hurried. As with most other skills, the development of effective communication skills requires extensive practice. Therefore, the learner must not be afraid to exercise what they have been working on in front of other people. The requirement to "put yourself out there" is one of the drawbacks and obstacles individuals face in the process of self-improvement. Many individuals find it difficult to comprehend how to improve their communication skills, and it is usually simple to see why. Many individuals find social interaction challenging and frequently detest communicating outside of their comfort zone. In other cases, individuals are oblivious that they could benefit from improving their communication skills. Consequently, the process of development requires an evaluation of the individual's current abilities, the identification of areas where change would be advantageous, and, most importantly, the selection of the most effective strategy for that development.

The first step in developing any corrective action plan is to comprehend communication abilities. Speaking, writing, reading, and listening are among its tactical fundamentals, but it also includes more specialized skills such as active and sympathetic hearing, appropriate bodily reaction and response, and context comprehension. After numerous hours of interaction with others, our communication skills progressively improve. Unfortunately, during this stage of development, we often acquire undesirable behaviors that are difficult to overcome.

THE BENEFITS OF EFFICIENT COMMUNICATION

There are too many and varied benefits of effective communication to list here;

they could even save your life, help you discover the love of your life, or save your marriage.

But in the business world, some of the most important benefits of enhancing your communication skills are:

1. Managing Your Employees

Staff management requires frequent, efficient two-way communication. If you are unable to communicate with those you supervise, your managerial abilities will be limited, and it could even lower employee morale. Communication is essential for a variety of duties, such as training, motivating, and allocating work to employees.

You may boost your team's motivation directly, indirectly, both indirectly and directly, or both indirectly and directly if you have excellent lines of communication with them. Simply stated, excellent communication skills can aid in people management.

2. Business Activities Outside the Organization

Whether you work for a corporation, the government, or another type of organization, you may have a job that requires you to interact with individuals outside of the organization face-to-face or over the telephone. In similar situations, effective communication skills represent both the corporation and the individual, making them even more crucial. The first pertains to the reputation of the organization or corporation, and the second to your professional success.

Increasing self-confidence

Improving your communication skills may be a crucial component of your long-term success strategy, as doing so will increase your self-confidence.

Developing your communication skills can also be beneficial in a variety of other aspects of your life.

Techniques for Enhancing Communication AbilitiesThere are numerous communication skills training programs available, and if you are not self-employed, your employer may be able to arrange a course or series for you. The type of course you should take depends on the reason for your need.

You may also take classes to enhance your written, verbal, and telephone communication skills. It genuinely boils down to selecting the most essential course in consultation with your employer, if applicable.

Speaking to employees or groups at every opportunity may be beneficial, as practice is also essential.

Three additional considerations are as follows:

Communication is a two-way street. You must do more than communicate with your employees. You must encourage them to be truthful with you. This may not always be easy; therefore, interpersonal skills genuinely shine in this situation. The ability to attend attentively is a vital skill and a highly valuable personal asset, in my opinion.

Always remember that the person with whom you are conversing is an individual; a group consists of individuals. I've managed over 100 employees in a variety of contexts, including my own company in the 1990s in England. It was essential to know and perceive each of these individuals because they were all unique.

3. If you have a large team or group of subordinates, it may be crucial to have a good memory, as effective management requires you to know each individual. Remembering them as a person when you need to communicate with them could reassure them and be advantageous for both of you.

Other forms of communication may profit greatly from memory. A good example is public speaking, where speaking from memory in front of a gathering significantly boosts one's effectiveness and self-assurance. The ability of a public speaker to create an impression is significantly diminished if they constantly refer to notes.

Memory may be an asset when presenting ideas, efforts, and suggestions to your elders. Possessing all pertinent information may aid your case and create a favorable first impression, making you appear knowledgeable and competent.

It is advantageous to learn how to improve communication skills because, under certain conditions, a person's communication skills develop slowly during their formative years and they lack the necessary social skills by maturity. However, it could be argued that our communication development influences our personality in numerous ways, a person's communication skills develop slowly during their formative years, and by the time they reach maturity, they lack the necessary social skills. However, it could be argued that our communication development has numerous effects on our personalities. In many instances, people would assert that their personality determines their communication manner and, by extension, their interaction skill set. Our communication manner and skills influence our public image and sense of self-identity. Stronger relationships with those around you will result from improved communication skills.

Even though a how-to template can help you become a more effective communicator, it is essential to remember that each template must be tailored to the user's specific requirements. Although the ultimate goals and objectives will remain critical and unyielding, you always have the option to construct your own how-to plan using the template's basic structure. Some self-improvement courses, for instance, require a specific amount and type of practice that may not suit your schedule or level of comfort. Self-improvement is a crucial stage in the process of human development, and actively striving to better oneself may result in a variety of advantages. Before deciding how to improve your communication skills, you must consider why you want to embrace change.

A healthy lifestyle includes effective interpersonal communication, so it is prudent to make an effort to improve. Consider how much time you spend daily connecting and conversing with others. Were you with a loved one this morning when you awoke? riding the transport to work with the driver? morning representative of the store? your cubicle neighbor as you discuss your most recent project? as your immediate supervisor provides you job-related instructions.

Chapter 9: Advantages Of Straightforward Communication

Customers and businesses frequently communicate via phone, email, and in-person interactions. To ensure customer satisfaction, you must use all of these communication channels, but face-to-face interaction is particularly important.

We also communicate frequently with colleagues and vendors, and our effective communication skills allow us to respond swiftly to requests and directives. This is significant because, in addition to affecting our own work performance, our reactions may also influence how well others perform at their employment. In order to enhance our communication skills, we must first acknowledge that stress and pressure are commonplace in contemporary society. This must be acknowledged as well as accepted as truth. The fact that your customer was late to work and a crucial meeting this morning because her dog was bitten by a parasite is not your fault. By the time she sees you, she is agitated and running late to collect up her children from school. However, if you take her behavior personally and respond defensively or violently, that is your problem.

Beginning at infancy, we are subjected to a variety of influences, and the person we become is a culmination of all of these influences. As we grow, we learn and adapt, beginning with the characteristics we inherited from our parents and over which we have little control. Our upbringing, level of education, and cultural heritage have all shaped who we are. Our manner of thinking is significantly influenced by our living environment.

Therefore, when we communicate with others, the ideas and emotions we express are dependent on our entire personal history. It is vital to bear this in mind when attempting to communicate effectively. A person considers their own thoughts and emotions to be extremely genuine and valid. Your neighbors' sentiments and beliefs that differ from yours are neither incorrect nor evil; they are simply different.

Effective communication is characterized by a clear understanding of the other person's needs, the capacity to share opinions in an informed manner, and the ability to reach mutually beneficial conclusions.

Chapter 10: How To Develop Confidence

Confidence is not innate; rather, it is something that is acquired through experience. If you observe someone with a great deal of self-confidence, they have labored diligently over time to cultivate it. Self-assurance is acquired, not innate.

Negative comments, business failures, and redundancies are a few examples of circumstances that can lower a victim's self-esteem. Even when they have good intentions, individuals can make you feel insecure by making offensive remarks.

In addition, there is self-doubt, which is the belief that you are unworthy of accomplishment and therefore unable to complete a task. The following actions are required for one to develop self-confidence:

Make an employee roster.

Creating an inventory of one's abilities necessitates noting the skills one believes to possess. When using this method, one must include every detail and leave nothing out.

Do you relate tales effectively? Do you endeavor for excellence? Do you chant while taking the shower? These items must appear on the inventory. Always consider the mentioned concerns, and be pleased of yourself. Do not be ashamed to boast about your achievements to your peers and coworkers.

Learn How to Acknowledge Compliments

Accepting compliments demonstrates maturity. The size of the contribution is more essential than its source. if the compliment is genuine and not something you were forced to accept. When complimented, respond with a heartfelt "thank you."

Instead of rejecting the compliment, believe in your own value and take delight in it. The compliments increase your confidence. Instead of assuming the praise you receive from colleagues or friends is sarcastic, have self-confidence and accept it. Accepting it after years of self-doubt may be difficult at first, but with practice, one can acquire mastery.

Education

Someone who takes pride in their knowledge or who reads many books will be confident. Increase your confidence by being aware of your surroundings, underlying issues, and familiar reading materials. Although it is not necessary to be an expert in the subject, having some knowledge of it can be beneficial. Discover the subjects that your coworkers and acquaintances find fascinating. This can be achieved through the study of fashion, politics, business, and athletics. Newspapers, periodicals, sports broadcasts, current topics, and newspapers all contain information.

Try a little risk and be receptive to novel concepts.

Embracing new ideas and embarking on new adventures can also contribute to one's sense of self-assurance. What matters is how you implement your concepts in practice. putting oneself to the test by traveling to different countries and engaging in activities such as eating Chinese cuisine, camping, watching NASCAR, and climbing mountains. At least twice per month, it is recommended to experiment with new concepts. Even if you don't appreciate one particular experience, don't give up quickly; instead, attempt a different one. Over time, self-assurance increases.

Exercising and Eating Well

One can maintain their body in a variety of methods outside of the gym. Morning jogs and swimming are two exercises that can be performed at home or in the neighborhood. Another option is to seek assistance from a gym trainer. A healthy diet can also improve mental and physical health. Consuming junk food can be detrimental to your health and even reduce your self-esteem. The regimen should include consuming large quantities of water and transitioning from unhealthy (junk food) to healthy (fruits and vegetables) foods. A nutritious diet and regular exercise can increase a person's self-confidence and pride in their accomplishments.

Alter the Individuals You Surround Yourself With There are certain people who make you feel consistently unworthy, voiceless, and full of negativity. Even if they are close acquaintances or family members, you must sever ties with these individuals. Replace them with someone who inspires hope and recognizes your potential. Someone who makes you feel secure and safe while in their presence. You owe it to yourself to attempt, even if making new acquaintances and parting with a longtime friend can be difficult. These new people have the potential to provide you with the encouragement you need to acquire confidence gradually.

Dancing for Personal Entertainment

When dancing, the brain releases a hormone that aides in stress management. You can dance in public or at home to your preferred music. It does not matter where you are as long as you have joy dancing. Instead of considering what others are saying, consider yourself. You will be adored for who you are; you may even astonish yourself.

Total Closet Renovation

Try on some ensembles that are stylistically distinct from your typical wardrobe. A change of clothes can be advantageous. Try on some new clothing, trousers, suits, shirts, deodorant, fragrances, and other accessories. Allow your loved ones to assist you in selecting ensembles that flatter your figure when you go shopping with them. Changing your complete wardrobe is still possible on a tight budget and without going overboard. When a person looks good, their self-assurance increases.

Try to accomplish more difficult duties.

This strategy may seem odd to a great number of individuals, but over time it increases one's confidence. By accepting additional responsibilities and undertaking additional labor, one tests his or her capacity. As a result of completing these assignments, you will encounter members of the organization.

Recognize and appreciate Others

This strategy involves being beneficial to those around you. As you work on your confidence, you realize that another person is experiencing the same problem. Be their guide and encourage them to build their self-assurance. Take the time to say thank you to your colleagues and family members who assisted you during your transition.

Adopt a positive attitude and never surrender

Don't give up when endeavoring to do something. Even if the exercise becomes difficult, make every effort to continue. Your desired outcome may be around the horizon. Every problem has a solution; you simply need to know where to search. When a person accomplishes something, they experience a sensation that increases their confidence.

Constantly negative thinking and being told that one cannot succeed can erode confidence. Continue to think positively about your situation and the steps you intend to take to rectify it. Don't give up, even if the objective you've set for yourself becomes more challenging along the way. Have confidence in your own value and aptitude. You become what you believe, so if you convince yourself that you are not attractive, not good enough, or weak and unable to succeed, you will become those things. However, if you consistently have positive thoughts about yourself, your confidence will grow.

Having knowledge.

Learn more about the duties you set out to accomplish, whether at home or at the office. Due to their confidence, someone who is well-prepared for an exam is more likely to succeed than someone who is unprepared.

Chapter 11: Never Evaluate Yourself In Relation To Others

Comparing your achievements or personality to those of others is typically not a wise decision. It is not a good idea to compare your attractiveness, lifestyle, place of employment, wealth, and job title to those of your family members, friends, or colleagues. It might result in stress and demoralization. Additionally, one's confidence may be negatively affected. According to 2018 research, those who experience envy towards others are more likely to have negative self-esteem than those who do not.

The research also revealed that individuals who frequently compare their lives to those of their peers are more likely to experience jealousy, which lowers self-esteem. Individuals who are more envious are more likely to have low self-esteem. Keep in mind that when you compare your abilities, skills, and expertise, you are performing poorly. The sooner you recognize that competition is not the only aspect of life, the sooner you will experience fulfillment and happiness.

Chapter 12: Identification Of Useful Information Sources

The identification of pertinent information sources is a crucial aspect of any research endeavor. With the proliferation of data sources, it is crucial to be able to rapidly and accurately evaluate the quality and relevance of information sources. The following stages can assist in identifying the most relevant and trustworthy information sources:

Determine the research subject: Before searching for information sources, it is essential to define the research topic precisely. This will aid in concentrating the search and identifying relevant sources.

2. Identify keywords: Keywords are terms associated with the topic of the investigation. These terms may include

subject-specific terms, synonyms, and related words and can be used to search for information sources.

Investigate information sources: Once keywords have been identified, the search for sources that may contain pertinent information can commence. This consists of academic journals, publications, conference proceedings, websites, and additional online resources.

After identifying potential sources, it is essential to assess the quality and relevance of the information contained in each source. This includes evaluating the credentials of the author, the source's publication date, its veracity, and its overall credibility.

As sources are evaluated, it is essential to maintain a record of the information sources. This may involve documenting URLs, citations, and the source's relevance to the research topic.

Sources of pertinent and reliable information

By adhering to these procedures, researchers can identify the most relevant and trustworthy information sources. This can help assure the success of the research project and the highest quality of the data collected.

Organizing your investigation is a vital component of any research project. It enables you to effectively manage the collected information, account for all data, and ensure that your project is completed on time and to the highest standards.

The first stage is to generate an outline of the research topics. This will assist you in identifying key areas of focus and dividing your research into manageable portions. Creating a timeline can also be beneficial, allowing you to organize your research and establish reasonable objectives for each section.

Create a filing system to organize your research materials. This could be a file cabinet, a database, or an online document management system.

Organize your research using labels and categories to make it easier to access and refer to.

Include the author, title, date, and any other pertinent information for any sources of information you use. This will make it easier to cite the source, give credit where credit is due, and ensure accuracy.

Maintain a record of your progress. This may entail maintaining a project journal, setting reminders, or monitoring your progress on a timeline. This will help you remain on top of your research and prevent you from overlooking important tasks.

It is essential to organize your investigation if you want to ensure a successful outcome. By taking the time to establish an organized system, you will be better able to access the necessary information, meet deadlines, and ensure that your project is completed to the highest standard.

Evaluating the Credibility of Sources

It is essential to consider the source's reputation, accuracy, timeliness, objectivity, and authority when determining its credibility.

It is essential to evaluate the reputation of the source. Is the source recognized within the field? Has the source previously published any reputable works? Are there any affiliations between the source and reputable organizations?

Additionally, it is essential to evaluate the source's accuracy. Exist any factual inaccuracies in the content? Are the content's claims supported by credible sources? Exist any prejudices within the content?

It is essential to consider the source's relevance to the present. Is this information current? Is the source still generating new content and active?

It is essential to consider the objective nature of the source. Does the source offer an objective perspective on the subject? Does the source present opposing viewpoints?

It is essential to contemplate the credibility of the source. Is the source an authority on the topic? Are the author's credentials listed? Are there any affiliations between the author and reputable organizations?

By evaluating a source's reputation, accuracy, timeliness, objectivity, and authority, it is possible to determine its credibility and determine whether it is appropriate for use in research.

The search for pertinent articles and publications

The search for pertinent articles and publications is an integral component of any research endeavor. To produce quality work, it is essential to locate accurate and current sources. The following suggestions will assist you in locating relevant articles and publications.

Initially, it is essential to define the scope of your investigation. Knowing what you are seeking and what information you require will help you narrow your search results. Once you have a clear understanding of the subject, use keywords to locate relevant publications. Look for both broad and narrow terms to obtain the most exhaustive results.

Second, use only reputable sources. It is essential to evaluate the credentials of the authors and publication. Ensure that the source is from a reputable institution or a current journal. In addition, seek out peer-reviewed sources, as they provide more reliable information.

Utilize multiple search engines to discover articles and publications. If you use multiple search engines, you may discover more pertinent sources. Consider using both general search engines like Google and specialized ones like PubMed or Google Scholar.

After locating pertinent articles and publications, be sure to peruse them carefully. Not all publications will be useful for your research; therefore, it is essential to read each one carefully to determine whether it is genuinely pertinent. In addition, be sure to take notes and assess the credibility and accuracy of your sources.

By adhering to these guidelines, you will be able to locate relevant articles and publications for your research assignment. With the proper resources, you can produce high-quality work and maximize your research.

Evaluation of Your Results

Our results analysis has provided us with a wealth of insight into our endeavor. We were able to identify areas of strength and improvement, as well as prospective risk areas and opportunities for further investigation. We also identified prospective cost-cutting and efficiency-enhancing opportunities. By thoroughly examining the data, we were able to adjust our strategy and allocate our resources more efficiently. Overall, our analysis improved our understanding of the undertaking and allowed us to make more informed decisions.

Application of Your Research to Your Subject

After conducting extensive investigation on your chosen topic, it is necessary to apply your findings in order to draw meaningful conclusions. Doing so will help you better comprehend the information you have acquired and provide you with a deeper comprehension of your research's implications.

To apply your research to your topic, you must first categorize your research. Categorizing your information will assist you in comprehending the various facets of your topic. After organizing your information, it is essential to analyze the data you've gathered. Consider the implications of your research and search for patterns or trends.

Once the data has been analyzed, it is necessary to draw conclusions. Consider what you've learned from your research and how it relates to the topic you're investigating. Consider how the information relates to the topic's larger context and make connections between the collected data.

Create an action plan for furthering your investigation using the conclusions you have drawn. Consider the additional data you require and devise a plan for gathering it. Consider how you can use the conclusions to construct an argument or make a suggestion.

By applying your research to your topic, you can gain a deeper understanding of your research's implications and use this understanding to advance your research. This will allow you to gain a deeper understanding of the subject and derive more meaningful conclusions from your research.

Chapter 13: Nonverbal Indicators And Their Influence On Communication

Nonverbal indicators, also referred to as body language, are nonverbal forms of communication that can convey a substantial amount of information. Included are facial expressions, eye contact, posture, gestures, and voice tone.

Nonverbal indicators can influence communication in various ways. They can support or contradict the spoken words, as well as communicate emotions and intentions. For instance, if a person claims to be joyful but their body language indicates they are angry or upset, this can create confusion and mistrust.

It is essential to be aware of nonverbal indicators, both in yourself and in others, in order to communicate and interpret effectively. Nonverbal clues can help you comprehend the underlying emotions and intentions behind a person's words, as well as help you communicate your own emotions and intentions more effectively.

Learning to read and interpret body language

Here are some guidelines for interpreting and comprehending body language:

Observe the facial expressions: There are numerous emotions that can be communicated through facial expressions, including happiness, sadness, anger, dread, and surprise.

Facial expressions are a crucial component of nonverbal communication and can convey a broad spectrum of emotions. The following are prevalent facial expressions that convey emotion:

Smiling: Typically, a smile indicates pleasure or friendliness.

A frown can represent sorrow, anger, or frustration.

This facial expression can indicate perplexity or concern.

Eyes that are narrowed can indicate wrath or suspicion.

It is essential to observe facial expressions in order to comprehend the emotions and intentions of the individual with whom you are communicating. However, different cultures and individuals may have various ways of expressing emotions through facial expressions, so it is not always possible to correctly interpret someone's facial expressions.

Observe variations in eye contact: Eye contact avoidance can indicate dishonesty, discomfort, or disinterest, whereas eye contact maintenance can indicate confidence, interest, or aggression.

Regarding eye contact, it is essential to recognize that people have different cultural and personal preferences. Some cultures may emphasize eye contact as a sign of respect, whereas others may regard it as an indication of aggression or disrespect. In addition, some individuals may struggle to maintain eye contact due to anxiety, discomfort, or other personal factors.

It is also essential to recognize that variations in eye contact can be influenced by a variety of factors, such as the topic of conversation, the speaker's environment, and his or her emotional state. For instance, a person may avoid eye contact when they are anxious, apprehensive, or uncomfortable, but may maintain eye contact when they are confident or enthusiastic about a topic.

When interpreting changes in eye contact, context and other nonverbal indicators must be considered. Although it can be a useful indicator of a person's emotions or intentions, it should not be the only indicator used.

Observe the posture and movements: Crossing the arms or slouching can indicate discomfort or disinterest, whereas an upright back and an open body posture can indicate confidence and interest.

Posture and gestures are significant nonverbal signals that can reveal a person's emotions and intentions. For instance, slouching or crossing one's arms may indicate discomfort or disinterest, whereas maintaining an open body posture may indicate confidence and interest.

However, context and other nonverbal signals must be considered when interpreting posture and gestures. When it comes to body language, people may have various cultural and personal preferences, and a person's posture and gestures may be influenced by a variety of factors, such as their emotional state, the surrounding environment, and the topic of conversation.

For instance, a person may slouch or cross their arms in response to distress or anxiety, but they may also do so when they are at ease or relaxed. Likewise, a person may stand up erect and maintain an open body posture if they are feeling confident or engaged, but they may also do so if they are merely attempting to appear confident or engaged.

It is crucial to consider the context and other nonverbal cues when interpreting a person's posture and gestures, and not to rely solely on them to determine their emotions or intentions.

Observe alterations in tone of voice: alterations in tone of voice can indicate alterations in emotions or intentions.

It is crucial to remember that body language can vary between cultures and individuals, and that it is not always possible to interpret body language accurately. It is also essential to consider the context and other factors that may be influencing the body language of a person.

Chapter 14: The Building Blocks Of Effective Communication

If you want to maintain open lines of communication with your children, you must do more than simply converse with them. To establish effective communication with your children, you must ensure that they comprehend everything you say. You can only effectively communicate with your children if you are confident in their ability to understand what you are saying.

There is effective communication between you and your child when there is a constructive exchange of ideas, emotions, and thoughts. When it comes to developing effective communication with children, puberty presents the greatest difficulty.

Even if your child and you have had a generally positive relationship, there is no guarantee that things won't become challenging once they reach adolescence. In actuality, the opposite is often the case. As a result, the majority of parenting experts advise parents to be prepared for this period so that they will be able to handle challenging situations in the future.

Parents can cultivate positive relationships with their children in a variety of ways. The first is beginning as quickly as possible. Express your affection and reassurance to your child even before they can speak. Continue doing this until your child is an adult to enhance communication between you and your child. But it is never easy.

You must recognize that children are constantly contending for parental attention.

Therefore, do not be harsh and interrupt your child with an annoyed tone if he approaches you from across the room anxious to tell you something, as this would dampen his enthusiasm. Instead of personalizing your child's comments, try to see the big picture.

You must recognize that children lack a mature sense of self-control. Therefore, you should not hold it against your child if he or she is condescending to you during an argument. When children are anxious or agitated, it is quite easy for them to speak harshly. When this occurs, instruct them to be courteous and polite.

In addition to criticizing his disrespectful behavior, you are teaching your child self-control through this action. Yes, you do not want your children to dislike you, but you also do not want them to seek support and affection from others.

Your relationship with your child will decline if you take things personally. The parent-child bond and communication channels are both weakened. Do not assign meaning to everything your child says or does. The most helpful thing you can do for them is to understand them as they navigate adolescence.

SETTING A POSITIVE TONE

When communicating with children, it is essential to use a positive tone, as this lays the foundation for healthy, constructive relationships. It is essential to remember that children are highly perceptive and frequently imitate the emotions and behaviors of the adults around them.

Here are some guidelines for communicating effectively with your children:

Try saying "Please use nice hands" instead of "Don't strike your sister." This prevents the use of derogatory language and promotes the desired behavior.

Children are still developing and may not always immediately comprehend or comply with instructions. It is essential to maintain your forbearance and refrain from losing it when others make mistakes.

Let your children know how much you appreciate and revere them. A straightforward "thank you" or "excellent work" can go a long way in boosting confidence and self-esteem.

Actively attend to your child by paying close attention to what they are saying while they are speaking. This demonstrates that you value their thoughts and opinions.

Validate their feelings: Even if you disagree with your child's emotions, it is imperative to acknowledge and respect them. As a result, they experience being heard and comprehended.

You can communicate effectively with your children by employing positive language, demonstrating patience, expressing gratitude, actively listening, and validating their emotions. By doing so, you can cultivate an environment in which your children can flourish and feel valued.

Chapter 15: Utilizing Clear And Brief Language

Parents and other caregivers must learn how to communicate plainly and directly with children. This type of language helps children comprehend what is being said and also promotes logical thought and effective communication. Parents and other individuals with parental responsibilities should communicate with children in a few crucial ways.

Use simple, easily understood language first and foremost. Because their language abilities are still developing, children may find it difficult to comprehend complex words or sentences. By using straightforward language, you can aid children in comprehending what you're trying to communicate and facilitate their responses.

Second, when communicating with children, it is advantageous to use precise, concrete language. Consider using concrete language and examples rather than generalizations or abstract concepts to make your point plain to children. For example, you could state "beware of the hot stove" instead of "be cautious." By using plain language, you can make it easier for children to comprehend the precise action you want them to perform and to follow your instructions.

Thirdly, it is essential to communicate with children in a language appropriate for their age and stage of development. Due to the fact that children are still acquiring their language, they may not understand or use certain words or phrases. Using age-appropriate language can help children comprehend what you are saying and encourage them to communicate more effectively.

Lastly, it is essential to communicate positively to children. Instead of using derogatory language or expressions, try to concentrate on the positive aspects of what you are saying. For example, you could say "please walk" instead of "don't run." Children who hear this type of language are happier and more likely to heed to you.

When communicating with children, it is essential to use basic, straightforward language to ensure their comprehension and promote effective communication. By using fundamental, clear, explicit, and positive language, parents and other adults who care for children can aid in their language development and help them gain a deeper understanding of the world.

Chapter 16: Observing And Displaying Interest

Parenting entails a variety of duties, including attending to and showing interest in children. It contributes to the growth of children's confidence and perception of self-worth. Children are more likely to open up and communicate with their parents when they feel heard and their opinions matter.

One way to engage children in conversation and demonstrate your interest in them is to give them your undivided focus. This involves putting down electronic devices such as computers and phones and concentrating solely on the child. Additionally, making eye contact, demonstrating that you are paying attention, and utilizing body language and facial expressions can be beneficial.

Another way to demonstrate interest is by asking children open-ended questions that encourage them to ruminate and share their thoughts and emotions. For example, you could question a child what their favorite part of the day was and why, as opposed to asking them if they had a good day at school. This makes children feel as though their opinions are valued and encourages them to speak more about their personal experiences.

Also essential is validating children's sentiments and emotions. This involves recognizing and accepting their emotions without criticizing or diminishing them. This fosters a sense of acceptance and support in children and teaches them how to express and manage their emotions appropriately.

When communicating with children, it is essential to be attentive, interested, patient, and understanding. Children may not always have the words or the ability to communicate, so it is essential to be patient and give them the time and space they need to do so.

A crucial aspect of parenthood is paying attention and showing interest when communicating with children. This can foster strong, healthy relationships between parents and children, and also makes children feel supported and cherished. By actively attending to and interacting with their children, parents can foster the confidence, self-esteem, and communication skills of their children.

MANAGING EMOTIONS AND STAYING CALM

It is typical for parents to experience a range of emotions when communicating with their children. Parenting can be challenging and emotionally charged, varying from pride and joy to irritation and rage. However, parents must control their emotions and maintain composure when communicating with their children for a variety of reasons.

Children rely heavily on their parents for guidance and support. They look to their parents to provide a safe environment and serve as examples of appropriate behavior. Children may experience uncertainty and confusion when their parents lack emotional control. They are unable to perceive what is occurring and believe they are to blame for their parents' emotions. As a consequence, children may experience shame and anxiety, which may have long-term negative effects on their emotional health.

In addition, parents are better able to interact with their children when they maintain emotional control and composure. When we are not overwhelmed by our own emotions, it is easier to hear and comprehend what children are saying. When we are calm, we can also respond more attentively and effectively. This is essential because it enables us to find answers and overcome problems as a family when confronted with challenging circumstances.

How then can parents maintain decorum and control their emotions when communicating with their children? Listed below are some potentially beneficial strategies:

Take a break: It is acceptable to leave the situation if you are feeling tense or agitated. Take a moment to collect your thoughts and take several long breaths.

Practice self-care: Ensure you are taking care of your emotional and physical requirements. This may involve self-care measures such as ample rest, healthy eating, and scheduling leisure time.

Communicate positively: When speaking to your children, avoid criticism and assigning responsibility. Instead, focus on answering questions and making progress.

When you have difficulty controlling your emotions, it is acceptable to seek assistance from others. Consider speaking with a trusted family member or close friend, or consider seeking professional mental health assistance.

It's not always easy to maintain composure and emotional control when communicating with children, but it's an essential skill for parents to acquire. By doing so, we can provide a nurturing and supportive environment for our children and serve as positive emotional regulation role models.

Chapter 17: Advocate For "Window Of Soul"

It is not by chance that our eyes are referred to as the "windows of the soul." Sometimes a glance can induce the desire to engage! Therefore, my friend, keep this "window" in mind at all times when conversing. I always bear in mind that the secret to success is "training your eyes to speak."

You should develop the habit of communicating your emotions and relationships through your gaze throughout the entire narrative, not just at the beginning and end. No matter where you speak, under what conditions, or with whom, having a soulful eye will make you appear considerably more alluring. To demonstrate my concern for the individual I'm speaking with, I always maintain a natural gaze.

As I just stated, it is crucial that you listen attentively to the following idea. Display interest with your eyes and focus with your hearing. In addition, bear in mind that while it is necessary to observe others, you should not do so in an annoying manner. This is quite disrespectful. Are you offended when someone stares at you in this manner? Simply shriek into the human stomach with our own bellies.

It is acceptable to occasionally glance away while speaking, but do not lift your head carelessly and pretend you are not looking. When you're at a party, avoid behaving as if you want to converse with someone more important than the person sitting next to you.

In this regard, I would advise you to pay attention to the language of your gaze as opposed to speaking without expression.

CONTROL LANGUAGE

Throughout court proceedings, the jury always pays careful attention to the accused's body language. Edward Bennett Williams, one of the most well-known attorneys in the United States, once told me that body language is crucial. Louis Nizer, Edward's companion, observed the defendant's hand and foot gestures and then matched them to the case circumstances in order to identify shared points of reference. complement to the profile.

Body language is an extension of spoken language, in my opinion. It is a fairly natural method to carry on a conversation. It has the potential to be a very effective technique because it is intuitive. However, it will not work if the body language is imitated or replicated with force. Even worse are instances in which others appear preposterous and amusing. Even though you are not a malicious individual, others will perceive you to be phony due to your pretension. Would you appreciate me if I imitated the voice and appearance of the esteemed Sir Laurence Oliver? And if one morning I attempted to imitate the speech patterns of Shakespearean actors, I would unquestionably be ridiculed. Therefore, I must constantly assess whether my speaking movements and posture are innate to me. It is my vernacular, even if it is imperfect. And I'm happy about it!

Thus operates sign language. The most natural experience with gestural communication can be derived from within. Be their steward! Speak from the heart and with honesty. Please refer to and implement a small portion of what you learn from others if you wish to acquire useful knowledge. Do not become an imitation of them.

SAY FORBIDDEN THINGS

Because modern society has become more receptive to new ideas and perspectives, the word taboo (taboo) has become less stigmatized. Numerous taboos have acquired traction in film, television, and literature because they are no longer fashionable. The 1990s are distinguishable from the 1950s and 1960s because the 21st century is more open than the 20th. The values of the past are not incorrect; however, they are no longer pertinent in the contemporary era. Rhett Buttler, portrayed by Vivien Leigh, remarks to Scarlett O'Hara, played by Scarlett O'Hara, in Gone with the Wind, "My lady, I did not curse anyone."

Their conversation has become routine since then.

However, certain topics are best avoided. Political and religious examples, as well as extremely sensitive and private matters. No matter how casual the conversation, you will never encounter someone who asks about your salary. Alternatively, you may have recently encountered a woman and have a compelling reason to inquire about her stance on abortion. Without a doubt, the other person will reciprocate your gaze with "bullet-shaped eyes."

To breach the taboo when speaking, you must first assess your relationship's closeness. We may discuss compensation with a close friend. It is also possible for a group of longtime acquaintances to discuss privately "thorny" matters such as gender relations openly and honestly.

Nevertheless, proceed with extreme prudence. Because the taboo topics you mentioned are inappropriate for the setting or intended audience, do not escalate the situation or cause disgrace through foolishness.

To initiate the proper topic and avoid getting "lost," one must be able to determine and evaluate the other person's comprehension of the issue. Are they enthusiastic about this event? Because relevance is currently the key to having productive conversations.

Chapter 18: Reasons Why Relationships Fail

Let's all concur that any worthwhile relationship requires effort. Relationships require an investment from us—to give when we don't have (cobbling together bail money for a brother), to show up when we are tired (helping a friend move after a failed marriage), to listen when we don't have the time (coaching a friend through job interview practice), and to recognize that presence is more important than flowers (sitting in silence, rubbing the back of a friend whose mother has died). Regardless of the nature of the relationship, navigating life and the experiences that accompany being in a relationship with another person can at times be excruciatingly difficult.

Just because we have acquaintances does not mean we understand how to cultivate them. Just because we are surrounded by individuals to whom we are biologically related does not mean that we understand what it means to be a family. Any relationship that has lasted for an appreciable amount of time has endured difficult and challenging circumstances that have affected the way its members interact with one another. This is the essence of being in a relationship. You weather the good times (the purchase of a new home, the birth of a child, a promotion at work, and the launch of a business) as well as the bad times (addictions, the tragic murder of a loved one, insolvency, a diagnosis of depression, and living with chronic medical conditions).

However, life-altering events can alter a person and linger like a cloud over the duration of a relationship, never disappearing but simply following. When this occurs, one or both individuals no longer know how to interact with the other. We have all encountered similar situations. A dear acquaintance, for instance, has been diagnosed with multiple sclerosis. The acquaintance becomes reclusive and less outgoing than they once were. As a companion, you are uncertain of what to do. You hurried over when you first heard the news and cried with them all night long. You offered support in the form of visits to your favorite restaurant, a movie night, and medical appointments. Nothing appeared to assist. However, the acquaintance has become secretive and private, unlike before the diagnosis. You have no idea what to say or do, but you want your friend back. The connection has broken down.

How about the recently liberated father from prison? Because he spent her entire adolescence in prison, he does not know his adult daughter. And the daughter is unfamiliar with her father. Neither knows how they should communicate with one another.

These scenarios are genuine. These situations occur to everyone. These circumstances make us feel uncertain. Close acquaintances become acquaintances. Which patriarch was just mentioned? His daughter calls him by his first name because it more accurately reflects their relationship. Usually, when we are uncertain, we remain in the current situation until something alters it. We are unaware of our role. We are unsure of what we are permitted to do or say. This is when tension begins to build.

We term it tension because the relationship is under physical or mental strain. It sneaks up on you without warning. In reality, we experience heartbreak because we perceive a sense of loss or hopelessness regarding something that will never be again. In addition, our stomachs become knotted whenever the individual is near or calls. We are concerned about the future. When we meet, will there be an outburst or deafening silence? We are outraged by what has already occurred, and we question why it occurred. In our minds, we rehearse various scenarios of what might be said or how we might respond. Because it is simpler to walk away and vow never to make contact again than to deal with feelings, emotions, and the unknown, we may simply ghost the person.

The Problem in the Room

This tension exists because something that is considered taboo occurred. In the context of a relationship, what does taboo mean?

Consider the following scenario: you have a companion who is having an extramarital affair. You think it is immoral, but who are you to judge? You were previously involved with a married person, so you feel that your opinion is invalid. But how do you proceed? Do you agree with it? Do you inform your spouse of the affair? Feeling guilty for harboring a secret, do you avoid your partner? Do you maintain secrecy? Do you attend double meetings when invited? Are you complicit in the affair if you concur? How does this relationship function now? You are unsure of how to manage the new dynamics of the friendship. There are so many unanswered issues.

Over the years, the friendship has endured far worse adversity, but it now appears different. Your friend anticipates that you will accept this "home wrecker" and go along with the plan. You speculate that your acquaintance is experiencing a midlife crisis. You have no one with whom to discuss the circumstance, and you do not wish to be involved. When it explodes, and it will explode, you do not want to be near the aftermath. However, you have been acquainted with this individual for over twenty years. So you appear, but less frequently. You communicate less frequently. And you surely do not discuss the incident.

What about the sister in the abusive relationship? You desire that she abandon her partner, but she will not. Every time she discusses the "relationship," you find it simpler to remain silent due to her unwillingness to change. It is agonizing to observe her suffering, and you feel impotent. To feel useful or protective in some way, you pack a "escape" bag in the event that you need to rush her out of the home. She is unaware that the suitcase is within the trunk. You have become accustomed to living with an agonizing secret. It negatively impacts the relationship. You are subdued, not as talkative. You typically wait to see what she will say or do before responding, as the abuse has become the focal point of her decision-making. Nothing remains the same in your relationship with her. You choose to remain silent about your emotions and the effect her situation has on you. You merely avoid discussing the abuse.

What about the pal who has fertility issues? What purpose does it serve? What are you to say when your acquaintance calls and says, "We've just had our third miscarriage"? The spouse has a child from a previous relationship, but he and his wife would like to have a child together. The wife has never given birth, and she feels inferior as a woman due to her inability to procreate. How do you assist your two friends? Unfortunately, when this circumstance arises between friends, most people avoid discussing anything related to infants. They avoid bringing up the subject of baby celebrations and are hesitant to reveal their pregnancy. Others may offer words of encouragement, such as "You can always try again," or inquire whether adoption has been considered. None of these statements is beneficial. Because the situation can be so awkward, you conclude that it is preferable to insulate them from the discomfort by not asking them about their fertility at all.

Obviously, this implies that there are now topics you do not discuss. It has acquired a stigma.

What about the relative who is an alcoholic in recovery? Do you conceal all the alcoholic beverages when he is around? You determine never to discuss anything related to drinking. In fact, you didn't even show him pictures from your last vacation because you went to a tequila factory and didn't want to "make him feel weird." To make matters worse, your aunt mentioned that your uncle is "on edge" and that she's concerned about him relapsing, so you remain silent about the entire situation.

What about the grandfather who sexually assaulted your sibling and cousin? The grandfather continues to attend family gatherings. Everyone is aware of what occurred, but no one has ever discussed it aloud. Your sibling and cousin should act as though everything is normal. In order for the family to "get along," there is a tacit expectation that everyone will act as if nothing happened. In reality, no one is getting along, and everyone is either puzzled or angry that everyone is acting as if nothing happened.

These scenarios are all plausible. At some point in our friendships and families, we will all encounter these types of situations. However, when these situations arise, we feel uncomfortable and unsure of what to say or do. Typically, we utter the incorrect thing or remain silent because we believe the topic to be taboo. We wish to communicate about our sentiments and the effect on the relationship, but we are unsure how. Moreover, we have no idea how the other party will respond. Thus, it is simpler to remain silent.

As a result of this silence, these situations go unaddressed, are avoided, and are kept hidden, resulting in significant tension and strain within families and between peers. There are numerous manifestations of the tension and strain. You can have members of your family adopt sides. Some want to discuss the elephant in the room, while others wish to keep it a secret, resulting in months or years of silence. It can lead to verbal and physical confrontations. Friends can cease conversing as frequently as they once did. Soon, days will become weeks, which will then become months. A few years pass before you realize it, and you've lost touch. You believed you would remain closest friends until the end, but you no longer communicate at all.

After a divorce has been finalized, some of us must determine who will be our friends. You don't want to choose, but you feel compelled to because each individual has insisted that you cannot be companions with the other. So, you friend one and unfriend the other without discussing it.

This is how prohibited subjects arise in all relationships. The tension between individuals in relationships and families is caused by taboo topics. The tension induces awkwardness, anxiety, confusion, sorrow, and emotional instability. We may even feel physically ill, perspire profusely, experience migraines, or shed tears. When these events occur in our lives and in our relationships, we experience a broad spectrum of emotions. Since we are ill-equipped to communicate with others in these circumstances, we opt to refrain from doing so.

Untouchable Subjects Are Exposed

Formally, the word "taboo" means "a ban or inhibition from social custom or aversion." While taboo is typically limited to offensive and inappropriate words, ethnic-racial-gender slurs, profanity, insults, etc., I extend the concept of taboo to include more than just words. The origins of taboo terms are situations, circumstances, and events. A taboo is something that is generally regarded as immoral and therefore is forbidden. Who, however, decides what is "morally wrong"? How even are principles defined? On what are principles based? Whose principles are they?

Consider the taboo subject of abortion, for example. Roe v. Wade was a landmark 1973 Supreme Court decision that established the constitutional right to abortion. On June 24, 2022, 49 years after Roe v. Wade, the Supreme Court ruled 5-4 to overturn the case. This is an unfortunate and unfortunate example of how one group can impose its morals on another, or in this case, an entire nation.

Prior to the decision and in its aftermath, particularly now that abortion is unlawful in some states, the mere mention of the word has caused cultural and social discord. Why? Because there are opposing beliefs about what constitutes the "right" decision. Some individuals believe a woman has the right to make decisions regarding her body. Others contend that the fetus must be safeguarded at all costs. Some have argued that abortion should only be permitted in cases of rape, incest, or if the mother's life is in peril, whereas others believe that these factors are irrelevant and the woman must carry the fetus to term. Some believe that the father is entitled to the embryo. In reality, there are numerous perspectives on abortion. Therefore, I believe we can all agree that abortion is generally considered forbidden. Because abortion has a lengthy and painful cultural and personal history, the majority of people do not wish to discuss it or express their opinion in public. Since Roe v. Wade was overturned, however, the topic of abortion is gaining more attention, and people are more willing to defend and express their opinions openly.

Practically speaking, a taboo topic is anything that carries a degree of secrecy if there is a belief that its mere mention would generate controversy, incite division, stigmatize certain people or groups, or cause drama due to the perceived "badness" of an individual's behavior, for whatever reason. This creates problems in the relationship because forbidden topics are identified based on an individual's judgments, which then inform decisions, which ultimately lead to actions that have an impact on the relationship.

This is how it occurs. Consider two individuals with distinct abortion experiences. One individual has an abortion, while another pays for their fiancée to have one. These two scenarios can play out very differently, but their communication outcomes are comparable. Consider first the woman who undergoes an abortion. It was a difficult decision for her to make, but she believes it was the correct one. She was raised in a religious household and considers abortion an immorality. She recognizes that it goes against her entire worldview. She is aware that she cannot possibly care for a child at this time. She is scarcely out of her own childhood. Moreover, the man who impregnated her is scarcely capable of caring for himself. The relationship was essentially an extended one-night affair. The only thought that enters her consciousness is, "I cannot have this child with this man at this time. If I have this baby, my existence will be forever altered.

A friend offers to transport her to the abortion clinic and spend the weekend with her to prevent complications and provide companionship. The acquaintance believes that having an abortion is wrong, even murder. Her thoughts rapidly shift to judgment. "How does she do it? How could she murder her child? How did I make acquaintances with someone capable of doing this?"

The woman having an abortion grieves for the unborn child who will never be born. Additionally, she is unsure of how her friend and others will evaluate her decision. She is wondering, "Will I ever be able to conceive again?" Am I causing irreparable harm to my body? Do I have the right to have a child after this? What if I am unable to conceive again? Am I destined for hell?"

Due to self-reproach and dread of judgment, silence is the preferred mode of communication. The acquaintance is also uncertain of what to do or say next. The companion finds it challenging to conceal her emotions. According to her, abortion is always immoral. However, their 10-plus-year friendship cannot cease because of this.

Neither of them is able to reconcile their emotions with what has occurred. Both have formed opinions about themselves and the other. For the sake of their friendship, they concur that it is best not to discuss it. In fact, they never again discuss the abortion. It has become a forbidden subject, and their relationship has never been as close as it once was because of this underlying problem.

Consider now the individual who pays for their intimate partner's abortion. It all began when he received the phone call, "I'm pregnant." His initial thought was, "Is it mine?" How far is she along? I utilized a prophylactic. So he contacts a friend: "I don't want to have a baby right now and I don't want to have a baby with her."

"She is pregnant!" What do I intend to do?"

"Have you asked her what she wants to do?""

You are aware I cannot ask her that.

Compas: "Why not?"

Because you are aware of how women feel about all of this.

"Bro, if you don't want to be owned by her for the next 18 years, you'd better figure out how to ask her what she plans to do." Plus, you are aware that the price will increase as she advances in her pregnancy."

"Right, right."

Friend: "You are aware of your obligations."

She obtains an abortion. He does not know how he feels about it because he was unsure if it was the correct action. However, his friend strongly advocated for the abortion. A portion of him feels conflicted because he will never meet his first offspring. He is furious with himself for listening to his companion and encouraging her to undergo an abortion. He calls his friend less and less after the abortion. He is dubious of how to hang out with the friend because the friend may inquire about the girl's well-being. The truth is that he wishes his friend to inquire about his health. He is aware that his friend has paid for the abortions of multiple females over the years, but this is all new to him and has been difficult. It has begun to give him nightmares. He mulls over what he will tell his prospective wife. Should he ever reveal that he financed an abortion? He believes that he cannot inform his friend everything he is feeling because he does not wish to appear weak or fragile. Therefore, he remains reticent about the abortion and does not bring it up again. Similar to the preceding example, a taboo subject has permeated the relationship and fractured it.

Both of these situations centered on the same taboo subject resulted in the same communicative outcome: silence. Because of implicit judgments, both parties decided not to discuss the abortion. Communication suffers when judgments and feelings of humiliation become a part of a relationship. No matter what the judgment is about, how the decision is rationalized, or what actions are taken, it is undeniable that the relationship has changed, and neither party knows how it occurred.

Chapter 19: Unspoken Regulation

Because it is an unspoken rule, the majority of people do not communicate about forbidden topics and do nothing to resolve the tension. How does everything originate in the first place?

Communicative behaviors are learned. We are taught them by our families ("Don't talk about your cousin's time in prison"). We acquire them from our culture ("Do not conduct business on the street"). We learn them from society ("It's impolite to ask someone [suspected of being an immigrant] where they are from"). We learn them from our peers ("We don't talk about molestation"). We learn them in school and on the job (e.g., "Don't ask anyone how much money they make"). The fact that we learned these behaviors from external influences does not obligate us to embrace and adopt them as our mode of communication. We can assume responsibility for our role in a relationship and communicate with intention. We can choose to communicate about the taboo topics that are causing tension in our relationships, thereby resolving the tension.

Just now, we discussed a few topics that many people consider taboo and that they typically keep concealed or in shame. It is fascinating that not everyone considers identical topics to be forbidden. Everyone has their own opinion regarding what is and is not considered forbidden. Although the dictionary definition of taboo is explicit, it is a highly subjective term. Subjectivity permits everyone to view the world through their own personal interpretation, biases, prejudices, and preconceived notions, and not necessarily through the lens of objective facts.

Sadly, this subjectivity is the reality in which people exist, make decisions, communicate, and function in relationships, regardless of whether or not it corresponds to fact. This creates an even greater issue. We never truly know what a person considers taboo until the situation arises. Even then, we may be unaware that the individual considers the situation to be forbidden because we do not discuss taboo topics. But we will know when something taboo has occurred because there will be awkwardness, estrangement, discomfort, shame, remorse, and secrets where there were none previously. Even more aggravating is that, because we rarely discuss taboo subjects, there is an implicit and tacit agreement to never discuss them. This results in another issue. Having a prohibited subject fester within a relationship is comparable to a cancer. It grows steadily and discreetly without causing discomfort... until it does. And when it does, it is typically catastrophic for the relationship (you have a major argument that results in you never speaking again) and for the people involved (you feel loss and sorrow). It can even affect those who are close to the parties involved, such as when a grandmother attempts to reconcile an estranged mother and son but is criticized by both sides and ceases to communicate with either of them.

www.ingramcontent.com/pod-product-compliance
Lightning Source LLC
Chambersburg PA
CBHW050237120526
44590CB00016B/2128